# My Beautiful Hungarian Home

*The memoirs of my life in occupied Hungary*

Words by John Abonyi
Written by Martin Abonyi

Published by The Solopreneur (Publishing) Ltd, Cedars Business Centre, Hemsworth, West Yorkshire WF9 4PU

The Solopreneur Publishing Company Ltd focuses on the needs of each individual author. This book has been published through their 'Solopreneur Self-Publishing (SSP)' brand that enables authors to have complete control over their finished book whilst utilising the expert advice and services usually reserved for traditionally published print, in order to produce an attractive, engaging, quality product. Please note, however, that final editorial decisions and approval to print reside solely with the author.

ISBN 978-0-9934527-4-1

Printed in the U.K.

*"There was a certain place that you had to aim for on the tank when you threw your Molotov cocktail. There was a two-foot plate that had inch diameter holes in it, like a grid. This was to cool down the engine. If you dropped it on this grid, the burning petrol poured into the engine and blew the tank up. We could see the turret of smoke blasting past us on its way skywards".*

# Contents

Foreword by *Martin Abonyi*

1. Before the Russians came

2. My dad's story

3. What changed after 1945? The seeds of
   Revolution

4. The Hungarian Revolution: My Story

5. My Escape to Austria

6. My New Life in England

# FOREWORD by Martin Abonyi

For as long as I remember, my dad's story about his life in Hungary has always been integral to our upbringing. It has always been there. Either in the background, in our sub conscience. Or at the forefront of our conversation and consciousness. My dad has four children. I am the youngest. I have two older sisters and one older brother. I think for all of us, my dad's story is seen as our inheritance, our legacy.

It's always been a story that we have all felt we needed to tell at some point in our lives. It's also a story that at some point in our lives, we have steadfastly defended, drawn courage from and drawn inspiration from. Whether we do that willingly or unknowingly only my brother and sisters can say for sure.

For me, in my early years, the story was told with immense pride, perhaps with a touch of drama as well, to my friends at infant and junior school. As I got older, and I realised the scale and sacrifice of the story. It became a reference point for certain aspects of my life. I think my sense of justice and iron-will, that occasionally appears, is a result of my heritage that this story demonstrates. I know that my brother and sisters have these references as well.

My dad sacrificed everything for what he believed in and ultimately had to stride out into a new world, leaving everything that he loved behind. That's courage.

At the age of 20, he had to leave his family, friends, and homeland behind and flee Hungary. His decision to leave Hungary was a tough one but also a decisive one. It was more of an escape than a migration. He was heavily involved in the uprising against the Russian occupation that broke out in the Autumn of 1956. This book is about one man's personal experience of what life was like in Hungary before and during the Russian occupation. It looks at how life changed dramatically for the majority of Hungarians when the Russians came. It looks at how this deprivation eventually sowed the seeds for the uprising that followed.

There's a first-hand account of the tactics used in the street battles that eventually ended in defeat for the Hungarians. It ends ultimately with my dad escaping to Austria as a wanted man for his involvement in the uprising. This book is a memoir of my dad's life and experiences for the relatively short time that he lived in Hungary. It's written almost entirely word for word from my dad's recollections.

This story is the result of hours of conversations and interviews with my father. It is written in the first person and from my father's perspective as he tells his story through these transcribed interviews.

*This book is dad's gift to us.*

# Before The Russians Came

*"Life was good in Hungary, but the changes started with the onset of war. As my dad was an officer in the army he had to go to fight when the second world war broke out."*

## Chapter One - *Before The Russians Came*

We had a wonderful life before the Russians came. My dad was a high ranking officer in the Hungarian Army. We lived in the army barracks in Sák when I was very young. My dad was in the cavalry. We had a good life, people generally, in Hungary before 1945, had a good life. We had three acres of land, and we used to grow produce, mainly vegetables that we sold in the markets. My dad also had a mushroom farm in Komáron. The mushrooms were kept in the dark in an underground cellar. When it was mushroom season, we used to sell two suitcases full every day in the markets. So we had the income from our food sales as well as my dad's income from the army. We had plenty of money, but most importantly, our freedom.

The farmers in Hungary owned their own farms. Whatever they grew, they had the right to sell it or keep it. It was their decision. There was no tax to pay the governments. What the farmers used to do was to send all the goods to the towns and cities markets every week. Chickens, eggs, vegetables, and so on. Whatever the goods were, they all got sold at a reasonable price. Everybody could afford to buy the goods. The farmers had plenty of food, and the money they got from the market sales, they used to spend on things like clothes and household goods. If they needed any extra livestock, they would pay for them out of the profits from the market.

I have fond memories of my life at the army barracks in Sák. I was only little, but I remember as my dad was in the cavalry so we lived near the stables. My dad had a horse called Sugar. It was a massive jet black horse. I wasn't allowed in the stables as it was strictly for officers. But one day I found my way in there on my three-wheeled bike. I rode around in circles in between the legs of Sugar on my bike until I was discovered and kicked out. I found out later that I was very lucky because Sugar was a very aggressive horse that would only let dad near her. I was lucky not to get kicked.

I also remember a few other lucky escapes when we lived in the barracks. When I was three or four years old, I used to watch my dad have a shave with his cut throat razor. I thought it would be a good idea for me to have one. My mum found me sat on the table covered in blood. I'd taken the razor from the kitchen and tried to give myself a shave. I was lucky not to have cut my head off, I had bad cuts to my neck.

I used to get about on my three-wheeled bike at the barracks. I remember one day riding straight past the guardsman straight onto a busy main road. How I managed to avoid all the traffic and get to the other side of the road, I'll never know.

I had fond memories of going to school as well when I was a bit older. One incident, in particular, sticks in my head. We had a lake near our school. One day the lake had been drained leaving a deep channel running through the middle. I think it must have been the course of an old river. Anyway, all the fish in the lake had swum into this deep channel as it was the only water deep enough to hold them. As I was on my way to school one day, I saw these fish in the channel and filled up my school bag with them.

Because I was on my way to school, I had to take the fish to school with me. When the smell got too bad I sneaked out of lessons and took the bag round the back of the school where they kept the livestock and hid them there. I got caught from the teachers at the end of school picking the fish back up. I got into trouble for that, but my mum still cooked the fish.

My mum was a fantastic cook. Because we grew a lot of our own food, my mum spent most of the day preparing and cooking different foods for us. As well as growing all our own vegetables, we also had cherry trees, peach trees, and plum trees. We made a lot of jams and syrups from the fruit trees. My mum also made a very nice cherry roll. She made a special flour, we called it double zero, I think it was semolina based actually. She mixed the flour with water and started to spread it out over a big round table that we had in the kitchen. She then put a white cloth over it and started to gently pull the pastry mixture towards the edge of the table. Eventually, the mixture was as big as the table and as thin as tissue paper. When this was done, she placed the cherries in the centre of the tissue-thin pastry and added a little oil. She then rolled up the pastry like a gigantic sausage roll and cut it into smaller portions so that they would fit into individual cake tins. Finally, putting them into the oven.

We also made all our own chutneys and sauces from the vegetables we had in the garden. We'd mix them up in a big wooden barrel, then have them in jars in the cupboard for all year round. We had many different kinds of homemade chutneys and homemade tomato sauce. We also had a well in the back garden, that not only provided water, but we also used it as our refrigerator as it was so cold down there. We would keep our milk, butter, and cheese down there.

We also used to keep our own livestock for food. We would rear one pig every year in the spring and fatten it up ready to be butchered in the Winter. This one pig provided us with most of our meat for the following year. When the pig was ready, we would ask a local butcher to come down and slaughter the pig for us. When the pig was butchered, he would put it onto a big wooden barrel with 100kgs of salt for a couple of weeks. He'd then check to see if the salt had drawn all the water and fluid out of the pig. If it had, he would then take the pig out of the barrel drain the fluid out, then put it back in with more salt. He'd do that for 6 weeks until it was ready to be smoked.

It had to be smoked in oak. We had to make sure that the oak was smoking and not burning. We'd smoke the pig for months. When it was ready, we'd hang the pig in the attic. It would keep fresh for the rest of the year. We also kept our own chickens, for eggs and meat. I remember watching my mum preparing the chickens. She would cut off the chicken's head and then it would run around the yard for a minute or so. She would then drain the blood off into a bowl, then pluck and gut it. The meat was beautiful, it was pure white meat. It was always my mum that slaughtered the chickens though, never my dad. He just used to watch.

Life was good in Hungary, but the changes started with the onset of war. Initially, dad's mushroom farm got taken over when the Germans came into Hungary. They used it for an ammunition dump and for heavy artillery. That was when we moved from Sàk to Tatabànya. As my dad was an officer in the army, he had to go to fight when the second world war broke out.

## My Dad's Story

*"When my dad came home in 1948 nobody recognised him. I answered the door and when I saw him, I shut it. I told my mum that someone was trying to break in."*

## Chapter Two – *My Dad's Story*

My dad was taken away in 1942 with the German
army when they advanced upon the Russian
army. My mum and I had to leave the house
where we lived in the army quarters, and we
went to live with my dad's sister. My mum had
to go out to work to keep me. She worked six to
seven days a week from morning till night to earn
enough money for clothes and food for the both of
us.

My sister was born in 1944 and when she
was born my dad's sister looked after her while
my mum was at work. My dad did not know he
had a daughter. I did not see my dad from 1942
until 1948. All the money that we had before
the Germans took my dad away to fight for them
was lost, along with everything else. The little
we had we took with us to my aunties. My mum
received dad's wages for so long, but after about
a year they stopped it. So mum had no income

whatsoever from dad. My dad had to change his name when he joined the army in 1920 because all the Hungarian soldiers' names had to finish with the letter I. Our original name was Alland, which was a German name. So dad changed his name to join the Hungarian army. All of my dad's family is called Alland.

When the war had finished, dad actually ended up in Manchester, England because the allied forces captured him. Because he was a high ranking officer, they asked him if he wanted to bring his family over to England. My dad said he wanted to go home. So my dad and another officer who was ranked above him started the journey home. They travelled home in a wagon pulled by horses packed with army surplus, like shoes, cotton, and other various materials. They got about 20 miles from home when they were captured by the Russian army. They were taken to six or more prison camps, but they were all full, so they were not accepted. Eventually, they got accepted at one. My dad dropped a letter on the floor just before he went into the prison camp. The letter was addressed to us and by a huge stroke of luck, it managed to find it's way to us. The letter told us that he was in Komáron prison camp. In the letter, my dad told us that he was being transferred to a Russian prisoner of war camp, and he told us the day that this was happening. My mum and I went to see him being taken away, first by wagons, then by railway carriage. We left my sister at home because she was too young. We saw all the Russian soldiers guarding the wagons and taking them into the carriages. That was the last time we saw him until he came home in the Summer of 1948. Because there were no letters allowed in the Russian prison camps, he could not write to us. We did not know if he was alive or dead, until he turned up on our doorstep in 1948.

He was sent to a concentration camp in Siberia, a Gulag. There were about 25,000 prisoners in the camp, by the time my dad left there were only 750 prisoners left. They were sleeping in massive cattle sheds with no walls. They were sleeping on straw. It was a very hard winter in Siberia, as it always is, and the conditions were very poor, with hardly any clothes and food. A lot of them caught dysentery and gastroenteritis. The prisoners were riddled with lice and bugs because of the straw. There were about 250 prisoners sleeping in the same barn as dad. Every morning about half a dozen of them didn't wake up, they were dead. The Russians had bulldozed a massive trench and every morning the dead were chucked into the trench. When the trench got full with dead prisoners, they just filled the hole in with sand, then dug another one.

One of the reasons why dad came home in 1948, was because of an incident that happened in 1942 during the war. The Germans had put him in charge of around 2,000 Russian Jews in Romania. Between Romania and Hungary the Germans were digging a trench around 200 feet wide and 200 feet deep between two mountain ranges. They concreted the trench hoping that if the Russians pushed the Germans back, the trench would stop the Russian tanks and armoured trucks from getting to Germany through Romania or Hungary. The Russians were pushing the Germans back that fast that they had no time to organise. The Germans gave orders to my dad to kill all the Russian Jews, to make sure that no-one was left alive to report to the Russians. My dad said he would follow the orders, but when the Germans left, dad told the Russian Jews and the Hungarian soldiers that it was every man for himself and that they were free to go. If they escaped good luck to them, but basically he set them free.

In the prison camp in Siberia where dad was, the officer in charge of the camp used to ask my dad to go to his house and help his wife chop logs for the fire, fetch water, and do a bit of gardening. It also helped that dad could speak Russian as well as German. So, every now and then he would get a decent meal at the officer's house. One day an officer from the Kremlin came to visit the camp. He recognised my dad and asked the officer in charge what his name was. He told him that my dad's name was Abonyi. The officer from the Kremlin said that he knew my dad and asked to see him. After the meeting, the camp officer was told to give my dad some decent clothes and food for a couple of weeks and then to release him. The officer from the Kremlin was one of the Russian Jews that my dad had released on the Romanian-Hungarian border. So that was how my dad got released from the prison camp.

When dad came home in 1948, nobody recognised him. I answered the door, and when I saw him, I shut it. I told my mum that someone was trying to break in. Mum came to the door, and she did the same thing, she shut the door.

He had long hair down his back and a long beard. His hair and beard were grey. When we finally realised it was my dad we sent for a barber to give a haircut and shave. He was there for most of the day trying to sort him out. When he cut his hair and beard, there were so many lice and bugs in his hair, that the hair that had been cut looked like it was moving on the floor. We then called in the doctor, and he said that he must not have anything to eat for at least two months, except for milk and chicken soup. Even the chicken and noodles had to be removed, he could only eat the stock. He could not have any bread or anything like that. The doctor said that a lot of people had come home lately and that they had been given a good meal, but because their bodies and stomachs had been so weak, it had killed them.

My dad had only been home about a week when the communists started to come around to the house from the town and try to get dad to join the communist party. My dad did not want to, and because of that, he couldn't get a job. He had to work on the farms with my mum and me. Later, he eventually got a job in Tatabànya as a miner, working on the top of the mine sorting out the coal. This was hard work for little pay. If he had joined the Communist party, he could have got a good job, with good pay and good hours. But because of his experiences in the prisoner of war camp in Siberia, he wanted nothing to do with communism.

My sister was four years old when my dad came home, and he'd never seen her. That was the first time.

## What Changed After 1945?
## The Seeds of Revolution

*"Standards dropped altogether, you could buy very little from the shops. You could only buy one loaf of bread per family per day."*

## Chapter Three - *What Changed After 1945?*
## *The Seeds of Revolution*

I was 9 years old when the Russians occupied
Hungary. As soon as the Russians came, they
took a lot of Hungarian prisoners. According to
them, they were war prisoners, but they were
really all civilians. They were replaced in their
jobs by the Russians. As soon as they were
replaced that is when the changes started. They
were taking farms away from people, to make co-
operative farms. All the prisoners that were taken
were put into a hard labour camp, working as
cheap labourers for the Russians.

The shops were full of food and clothes before
the Russians came. Everything that was made
in Hungary was for the Hungarians. When the
Russians came all our goods were exported to
Russia. People were happy before 1945. We
would have days of eating, drinking, and being
merry, but all our good times seemed to stop

when the Russians came. They put a lot of tax on the farmers, so we didn't have much money or livestock. Sometimes the output did not meet the high demands of the Russians, so the farmers had to try and make it up the next year on top of the current year's demands. So each year the output would fall due to the high demands forced on us by the Russians.

To start off with, the Russians would send some of their people out to start stocktaking. They wanted to know how much livestock the farmers had. They told the Hungarian farmers that they had to give so much of their produce to Russia. If you had cows, you had to give away so much milk. If you had chickens, you had to give away a certain amount of eggs. If you had sheep, you had to give away so much of the wool away. All of this was for nothing, so we were losing money and produce at the same time. The fields you owned, the Russians got a share, and if it was a bad harvest and you only met half of your target, the rest of the target would be added to next year's harvest. The farmers got fed up with this as they were working for nothing most of the time. Most of the farmers left their farms to go into industry.

Also, when they fetched in the co-operative farms, the tractors ploughed the fields too deep and after a year or so the soil was no good. The Hungarian farmers had used their own livestock's manure to fertilise the land. So every five years, the nutrients in the soil were replaced. We could not use these methods when the Russians came as most of the livestock was taken by them. A lot of our remaining livestock suffered in the winter due to the lack of food which had been taken by the Russians.

Standards dropped altogether, you could buy very little from the shops. You could only buy one loaf of bread per family per day. If you ran out of bread in the afternoon, you had to wait until the following day to get some more. They only brought so many loaves into the shops, so you had to queue up. People queued all night, and only the first thousand or so got the bread. The other had to wait until the following day. You could not get any sugar. The only item that you could get easily was shoe polish, shoelaces and salt. It was also hard to get things like clothes, because all the clothes and furniture etc., was all shipped out of Hungary in big wagons and lorries to the Russian big cities like Stalingrad, Leningrad, Moscow, and Kiev. Everything that was produced in Hungary including cars, lorries, heavy industry, coal, minerals, bauxite, copper and uranium, etc., it all went to Russia. So there was not much you could buy in Hungary anymore. The living standards went down altogether.

In 1946, after the Russians had been there for a year, everything started to go bad. The shops were empty, there was hardly any food. They changed a lot of people, such as teachers.

All the regular teachers had been changed to the teachers that the Russians themselves had brought in. They took away speech rights, so there was no free speech or free writing. People started to disappear. I realised after a year that communism wasn't as good as the Russians made out.

The lessons at schools changed when the Russians came as well. Firstly, they brought in Russian as the compulsory language. Everyone had to learn Russian. The few remaining Hungarian teachers, those that hadn't been replaced, mainly the older teachers, could not argue or express an opinion about politics. Every two or three weeks they had to attend meetings about Russian politics. They also had to inform the Russians if anything had gone off in school, like an argument or political debate or conversation.

A lot of people were scared, so you had to agree with the Russian politics and just keep your personal views to yourself. You could get help from the teachers, depending on what lesson you had. Any lesson to do with politics, you just had to listen and not say much. The new Russian teachers would tell you that everything before 1945 was bad and wrong. They told us that the stuff that they were teaching us was much better than before and that we had to reform. You did get help in all your other subjects, just not politics. We had two hours of politics every day at school. They tried to tell us how bad things were in the West. They said that people in the West were worse off us under capitalism. They told us that in a capitalist regime everybody works seven days a week for hardly any money. They told us that housing was very poor and that there was no freedom whatsoever. They brought in the people's radio which was on top of every lamp post on every street. It broadcast non-stop propaganda. People had no choice but to listen.

Basically, freedom was taken away from

everybody. To start off with, when you left
school the first job you got you were given a
work permit, a bit like a passport. If you did not
like the job for any reason, you could not leave
unless the boss said you could leave. If you left
on your own free will to go to a different job, the
first thing the new employer would ask for was
your work permit. If you had left, the previous
boss would not give you your work permit unless
he agreed to the move. If you did not have your
work permit you could not get a job anywhere.
This meant that you had to go back to your old
job and be put in front of a tribunal to decide
your punishment. The punishment was anything
from six months to six years work for half wages.
It was not very often that the sentence was six
months, it was more likely six years. All they were
after was plenty of cheap labour so they could
keep up with the West. That is how they kept up
with the West in the arms and space race and
why they manufactured so many tanks, ships,

and armaments, because of the cheap labour.

The scientists who worked in the communist states were not like those that worked in the West. They had no bargaining power with the things that they invented or created. Under communism, they were all put in a special institute with all their families. There was no free movement or holidays to other parts of Russia and other countries. They could not leave the Institute. They were under constant surveillance and were told exactly what to do. There was no bargaining or freedom like what the other scientists in England and other Western countries enjoyed.

Soldiers used to patrol the streets. You were not allowed to be on the street in pairs, or carry cameras around, especially at places like train stations, communist buildings or airports. You were not allowed to be in groups. The soldiers walked up and down the streets in pairs with machine guns. You were not allowed to stop on

the streets in groups of three and four and hold
a conversation, as the soldiers wanted to know
what you were doing and what you were talking
about. They would ask for your identity card.
Everyone in Hungary had been issued with an
identity card and if they caught you on the street
at any time of the day without the card, that was
the end of you, no-one saw you again.

You could not come and go as you pleased. To
start off with they had what they called gatemen.
When you went into the entrance of a big block
of flats, there was an office with a big window.
There was a guard there twenty-four hours a day
and seven days a week. He had a two bedroomed
flat on the bottom floor which was free. His job
was similar to that of a hotel receptionist. When
you went out you would give him your key and he
hung it up on a numbered board. He also had a
log book and you had to tell him where you were
going. He registered the time that you went out
in the log book. If you came back a bit later than

what you said, there were a lot of questions about where you had been, who you had been talking to and what you had been doing in that extra time. They also went up into your flat if they were a bit suspicious and put a bug in it. So when your family came home in the evening and started talking, they listened into your conversations. If you said anything that they didn't like, they would come for you in the middle of the night. Usually, around three in the morning and that would be the last time anyone saw you.

There was no such thing as a courtroom or a fair trial in communist Hungary. There were no lawyers, barristers, or counsellors, to ensure a fair trial. What they did in a lot of cases was to frame you. They planted incriminating evidence on your property, like guns for example. They would then come round the next day and say that you had been hiding weapons and that you were working for the underground movements and working against communism. They would then take you to a police station, where two soldiers would escort you into a room to be questioned by the AVO or KGB officers. They would then tell you that the people of the Hungarian Republic find you untrustworthy in a communist regime and therefore as punishment they would put you into a Russian hard labour camp, and that was the end of it. With that, all your family would be evicted from your flat and then punished.

One of the biggest issues in communist countries was propaganda. To start off with, in schools, industry and the military, there were a compulsory two hours a week, where they taught you tactics on how to take over the West. Instead of using nuclear missiles or starting a war, they taught us how to take over the West by using propaganda and politics. This included sending as many spies to the West as was possible. They would obtain good jobs in high places with authority where they could get valuable information and gain influence over a workforce. A good example would be a Union leader in England, that way they could have a lot of influence over the workforce. Also, white collared jobs such as civil servants and working for governments. This way they could gain valuable information and have access to classified documents. Leaflet campaigns to spread propaganda was part of the plan.

When I was working for International Harvesters in Doncaster in 1958, there was a man stood outside the factory issuing leaflets. The leaflets were promoting the communist way of life. They said that in communist countries they have a 36-hour working week and the average wage was a lot better than in England. I knew that this was simply not true. It was a 48hr working week, even the schools were six days a week and 48hrs. In communist countries, you were only allowed a week's holiday or a fortnight at best. The pay, even in the mines, which was the best pay, was about £10 - £12 a week. They were trying to cause unrest and disturbance among the English workforce. When a strike occurred in England, Russia would send the Union leaders and administrators money so the bosses would still be getting paid, while the workforce got nothing. England, at the time, like Russia was an industrial country and they relied upon a big export market. They needed to export more in order to import food and other goods into the country, the stuff that England wasn't self-sufficient in. So they needed to export more goods than to import to avoid a trade deficit. At Harvesters, by striking, they lost all their orders, because if the customers did not receive by the deadline, they would cancel the orders and take it to another company who could produce it on time. It was not good business to be involved with a company that strikes all the time. A case of this kind happened at the Harvesters while I was there in 1962. A company in Egypt had ordered 2000 tractors, as soon as the workforce realised that it was a big order, there was pressure from the Union bosses to ask for a pay rise, £15 a week I think it was. When the raise was refused, we went on strike and could not complete the order. The order was cancelled and taken to Germany instead. In the end, companies were losing orders, and people were losing jobs.

At the same time, the Russians were telling people at home and in Hungary and other communist countries, how bad the conditions were in Western countries. They told us that they had poor living conditions and had no possessions etc. They broadcast this news from nearly every lamppost in the street on the people's radio. The people's radio broadcast 24 hours a day and seven days a week. It told the Hungarians that the standard of living was far better under communism than it was under capitalism. The people's radio was the only radio station in Hungary after the Russians came. It was obvious what kind of news would come out of it. They only told you what they wanted you to know. A lot of the broadcasts detailed the performances of Hungarian industries. For example, they would tell you how many tonnes of coal one mine had produced, and that this should be the target for the other mines that had not achieved this target. The same went for other industries and agriculture. When the Russians got people to strike in England, it made priority news on the people's radio. They made a big point about it, saying that the people were striking again in England because of the poor conditions under capitalism. They said that English families had no clothes, nothing to eat and that in Winter they were freezing and starving. They made a big deal out of this, it was big news on the people's radio.

The Russians used to take the English Union leaders to Russia for a diplomatic holiday. They took them to the Kremlin in Moscow, that was the only place that the Union leaders would stay. Obviously, the Kremlin is the place where the Politburo, officers and people in power were, so the living standards were high, probably better than in England. Moscow, Leningrad, and Stalingrad, were rich cities because of all the materials and goods that came there from all the other communist countries. These three cities dictated half of Europe. They made sure that the Union leaders were well fed and looked after. When they took them on visits, they never took them to any of the working class areas. They never saw the true Russia. According to the Russians, the places that the Union leaders were taken to were working class and typical of all communist working class areas.

Visitors were treated the same way in Hungary too. My wife went to Hungary in 1967, and she got this special treatment. In Budapest, there was a special shop where you could buy everything you needed. But only the Russian KGB and Hungarian AVO could buy anything there. You were not allowed in without a pass. The Russians gave my sister a pass when they learned that my wife was coming so she could buy food from this shop. They did not want my wife to go back to England and say how bad the shops were in Hungary. What they did not want was bad publicity. So, my wife could go to this shop and buy all the top quality foods, what the ordinary Hungarians had not seen since 1945. Other than this special shop the only meat you could get was fish. There was a butcher's shop in the town of Tatabànya. All it had was a big fish tank with lots of different types of fish in it. You just pointed to the fish that you wanted and the butcher would catch it and hit it over the head with a wooden mallet and then wrap it up for you. That would be your meat for the week. The Russians were good at hiding things from Western visitors and good at putting down Western countries by the use of the people's radio.

I was 15 when I left school. After school, I got

a job as a bricklayer's labourer. I was working there for about two years when I heard that there were places free at the mining college doing engineering. They were recruiting people to work in the mines. I applied for the college because my results were good from school I had a chance of getting in the college. I got the place and started in the Autumn of 1954. I went to college 220 miles away in a place called Kö Könyos. The college terms were similar to the structure in England. I only went home at Christmas, Easter, and during the Summer. For the first month I was at college five days and then one day working down the mine. Even college was 48 hours a week and six days a week. Monday to Friday I went to college and Saturday I was working down the mine. We started at 8am and finished at 4pm for college. Down the mine, the shift system was the same as in England. 6am till 2pm, 2pm till 10pm and 10pm while 6am. But for the first six months, we were on the shift 6am to 2pm, every

Saturday morning. The following six months were three days at college and three days down the mine. The next six months was one day at college and five days down the mine. The final six months, which completed our two-year course, I was six days down the mine. On Sundays we did sports activities, playing football against different colleges or mining teams. When I finished the two-year course, I got offered a good job provided I joined the communist party. I refused to join the communist party, so I did not get the job. When I started the two-year course, they promised me that when I finished my course, they would transfer me to Tatabànya, where I lived. Tatabànya is the biggest mining town in Hungary. This meant that I wouldn't have to be 220 miles from home. But they never transferred me, they wanted me to stay in Kö Könyos, which I did not want to. So I left and went home.

I got a summer season job in my town threshing barley, corn, and wheat. I worked

there until the end of August, then got a job
in Tatabànya, sorting out fruit and vegetables.
The warehouse distributed its goods to different
shops. I also worked with my dad for a while,
bailing straw for a textile company. We put the
straw through a thresher when it was three
feet high and extracted all the oil from it. When
we bailed the straw, we put it in big concrete
containers with rubber sealed doors. We then
turned on the steam pipe and let the pressure go
up to two hundred pounds per square inch. This
softened up all the straw, we would then put it
in a big warehouse to dry. We would then put it
through a machine that broke all the hard casing
of the straw off and it would just leave the inside
bit, which was a fine white silk. Then we would
send it to a textile mill, and they would weave it
and make yarn out of it. Then they bleached it
white, then dyed it different colours.

In the Winter when the work at the textile
factory was slack, we used to work at the forestry.

The forestry commission would mark out an area of around two or three acres and mark the trees that had to be cut. We had to cut them down with a double-handed saw and then take all the branches off, which we were allowed to keep. We then cut the tree itself into segments of a metre length. We would then split the segments in half with two steel wedges and a seven-pound hammer and then into quarters. If we cut a hundred cubic metres of wood in a month, we would get a third. So we would get thirty-three cubic metres of wood if we met that target, as well as the branches. When we had finished, all the stumps that were left in the ground, were ours as well. So we used to borrow two shire horses from the farm where I worked in the Summer and attached two big bull chains. We dug around the big stump and dug up the roots as best we could. We then tied the chains around the stump and attached them to the horses and they pulled the stumps out. We then took the stumps home, dried them, then split them with steel wedges and hammers to use on the fire. The branches I would chop into two-foot lengths and bail them with wire. We then used to make our bread in the big oven that we had and use the branches to light the fire. We used to burn them two or three bails at a time. The branches warmed up the oven so we could bake the bread.

# The Hungarian Revolution: My Story

*"So we took the sixty or so AVO officers who were still in uniform into the yard. We tied their legs together with belts and then hung them on the hooks."*

1. John Abonyi in Hungary 1938
2. John's Dad in Hungary 1939
3. John Abonyi in Hungary 1954
4. Hungarian Passport 1954

5. *John in England 1957*
6. *John's sister Magdi with his two daughters in Hungary 1967*
7. *John's Dad and Sister in Tatabariya 1962*

DADDY AND DIANE IN THE PARK.
1966.

8. John with his Mum, wife and two daughters in England 1969
9. John with his Daughter Diane 1966
10. John at Great Yarmouth 1982
11. John, Margaret and Judy 1983

12. *John and Margaret at Great Yarmouth 1986*
13. *John with his daughter Tracey and Grandaughter Chloe 1994*
14. *The Abonyi Family 1996*
15. *John and his sister Magdi in England 2014*

**Chapter Four -** *The Hungarian Revolution:*
*My Story*

Because I could not get a job in my trained
profession as I would not join the Communist
party, I was glad when the revolution broke
out around the 11th October. I got called up
for the army on the 6th October on my 20th
birthday. Twenty was the age of national service
in Hungary, you spent two or three years there
depending on what part of the army you were in.
I was only in the army a couple of days before
the revolution started. They did not even have
time to cut my hair. In communist armies, the
first thing they do is shave your head for the first
six months, that is how they knew you were a
new recruit. This is so if you were identified in
town without a pass, they knew who you were. If
they found you on the street, or in the town, or
anywhere else, they took you back to camp and
put you in jail for six months.

That morning we woke up at about 9am, which was unusual, as they would normally call you about 5am. Everyone had to go down to the courtyard in their shorts and trainers to do morning exercises for about half an hour. Even if it was raining or snowing. Then you got washed and dressed and set about your usual routine. But on that particular morning when we go up there was nobody about. We knew then that something had gone wrong.

About a month before the revolution broke out, all the students were talking about political affairs more freely and were hanging around in groups on street corners which were strictly forbidden. Things had gotten slack as far as the oppression was concerned. I had a feeling that something was going to happen. On that morning we found out that the Prime Minister Matthias Rakosi and all the AVO and KGB officials had all got on planes and fled Hungary. This left the army without any commanding officers. In all the towns and cities the main AVO and KGB buildings and jails were without officers. We had no orders or commands so the only thing we could do was to go home. So I went home to Tatabanya, where I lived. At around 11am that same day I found out that all twenty-five mines in the Tatabanya area had stopped production. It was a national strike. A national strike had not occurred since 1945.

Naturally, the streets were full of excited and curious people, talking about the events and generally hanging around. It was chaos. Later on that morning a lorry load of students arrived from Budapest and began distributing leaflets to everybody. The leaflets contained ten points that the students wanted in order to gain freedom for the people again. One of the points was for the Russians to pull their troops out of Hungary. There had been around 50,000 Russian troops in Hungary since 1945. They had been here that long that they had become used to the Hungarian way of living, which was generally better than in Russia. The crowd became excited, and we followed the students to the AVO headquarters in Ujvåros, which was in another area of Tatab'anya. The headquarters was a fourteen storey building which had a large concrete wall at the back of the building, which had no windows in it. Surprisingly, the AVO officers that were left let the students in. The students appeared on the balcony to speak to the crowd, which now contained about 20,000 to 30,000 people, they were all stood in the street.

The speaker, who was a girl, started to read the ten points that had been drawn up. While she was speaking, someone shot her dead from inside the building. This aroused the crowd, which quickly became angry and started to storm the building. They could not get in because the door was a two inch thick, high-density steel rolling door which was operated mechanically from inside.

Because I was in the army, me and about six of my friends had access to lorries and trucks. I had taken training in driving lorries about a year earlier, so we went down to Alsógalla at the other end of Tatabanya where the army supplies were. At Alsógalla they had lots of Scammel lorries in which they used to transport tanks. By this time a lot of people had followed us. We also found an ammunition dump at Alsógalla. It was a big underground concrete building. From the top it just looked like grass, you would not know that it was an ammunition dump. We found that there was plenty of ammunition in there, so we broke open all the doors and the people that followed us stocked up on all the weapons. We got machine guns, grenades, boxes of bullets, etc., and loaded up the Scammels. We put them in the lorries and drove back to the AVO building. We backed the lorries up to the doors and smashed them down. The people were then able to get in.

We found out that all the AVO officers were in

the building because they lived there, they never came out. They had a small room each, with a bed, wardrobe, and little sink in it. The doors were leather padded, sound-proofed doors. We found a lot of torturing equipment in the building, which they used to torture the prisoners. We got all of the AVO out of the building. The revolutionaries threw a lot of the AVO officers out of the windows where the crowds were waiting for them. They killed the AVO as they landed. We found a lot of AVO hiding in wardrobes and under beds, etc. We took about fifty or sixty of the AVO officers down to the courtyard, which overlooked the big concrete wall which was the back of the AVO building itself. There was a string of hooks on the wall. These were used by the AVO officers to torture prisoners. They would hang them up on the hooks in the summertime, they would tie a belt around their legs and hang them up when it was red hot. They were left there for a couple of hours as punishment. We also discovered that the building had four storeys underground. This was where the prison cells were, they had no light, no heat, and no bed. There was just enough room to stand, that was where they kept the prisoners. Where the prisoners used to stand there was a two inch wrought iron grid. This was where the sewer system used to run under the prison cells. All the stink from the sewers used to come up into the cells. We also found under the building at the end of the cell passage a big room that held a great big mincing machine. They would put the prisoners in there and mince up their bodies. They then let their minced up bodies go into the sewers underneath all the other prisoners and out into the drains and rivers. Once you were taken in the AVO building, no-one saw you again.

So we took the sixty or so AVO officers who were still in uniform into the yard. We tied their legs together with belts and then hung them on the hooks. We then got some petrol out of the

AVO garages, they had their own garages for their cars and lorries. We doused them with the petrol and set them on fire. What we did not know was that on the four corners of the AVO building there were four surveillance cameras, and they had filmed our actions. The cameras were used to keep an eye on the prisoners as they exercised in the courtyard. That was how they knew if the prisoners were talking to each other or handing papers over to each other or anything like that. So everything that we did in the courtyard was captured on film.

From Tatabànya we went to another town, it was a mining town called Oroszlàny. There were four big prison camps in Oroszlàny. These were for people who were sentenced to 30 to 45 years of hard labour. They had to work seven days a week for 12 hours a day. They worked mainly down the mines on 12-hour shifts. When one lot of prisoners finished their shift, another lot went down for 12 hours. They got eight ounces of bread a day plus a pint of water, that is all. There was no proper bedding or lights, they had to sleep on the floor. There were no showers either. There was a big electric fence all around the camp which had a 25,000 current running through it. There was also watch towers every fifty yards with searchlights on the top of them, as well as around the clock guards with guns. There was not much hope of escaping.

So, when we went to Oroszlàny, it was about five or six o'clock in the afternoon. We released all the prisoners and shot the AVO and KGB officers and guards that were there. By that time it was around 9pm, so we collected all the lorries, buses, and jeeps that were in the town and all the people that were behind our cause, there was around 20 - 25,000 people. We organised them onto all the buses and lorries etc., to form a massive convoy. We then set off to Budapest, which was about 30 - 40 miles away. We were planning to meet up with the revolutionaries in

Budapest.

When we left Oroszlány to get to Budapest,
we had a convoy of about 25,000 people. We had
two men who had emerged as the leaders of the
group, we knew who they were as they drove
a Skoda. We were a bit dubious about them,
they seemed too well dressed to be ordinary
Hungarian civilians. They emerged as our leaders
as they said that they knew the best way to enter
Budapest, and they had a rendezvous point
with the Budapest revolutionaries. We mainly
travelled by night to Budapest. About five miles
from the outskirts of Budapest, we stopped at
a petrol station to fill up the buses, lorries, and
cars. When we had filled up the vehicles, we were
waiting for our two leaders to give us orders to
move on when we realised we had lost them. The
Russian car had gone. So we carried on without
them. This meant that we had to travel on a long
and narrow road into the capital. This road was
in a valley, it had hills and forests surrounding it.

When all the vehicles were on the road, stretching miles back. The Russians attacked. They blew up the first two vehicles and the last two vehicles in the convoy. This meant that all the vehicles in the middle were trapped and unable to move. Then the Russians opened up with machine gun fire and grenades. By the time all the vehicles managed to stop a lot of the vehicles had crashed into each other because of the Russian strategy to blow up the first two and last two vehicles in the convoy. It all happened in a split second, we did not expect it. From then on it was easy for the Russians. They had the cover of the trees, the advantage of the higher ground and a perfectly planned ambush under the cover of night time. We were stunned and unprepared. It was mayhem. We lost most of our convoy on that road.

I managed to escape through the hills and forests. I was only a mile away from Budapest itself, myself and the other survivors all managed to make it to the outskirts of Budapest. When we re-grouped, we found that there were not many survivors from the convoy. We holed up for the night in Budapest and in the morning we started to re-group.

There was a Russian army that had been in Budapest since 1945, we knew of this army and how they had become educated and accustomed to the Hungarian way of life. They would not be so affected by their own propaganda as they were by and large living as Hungarians. We knew that a lot of them had tried to escape. We had heard the stories of them defecting from their base camp. There were 50,000 men and two tank divisions in Budapest which made up the Russian army presence. Obviously, when the defectors were caught, they were shot. Because all of the commanding officers had been pulled back to Russia when the revolution started a lot of the Russian soldiers mixed with the revolutionaries. They would leave their tanks and ask us for civilian clothes. Luckily for the Russian defectors, Russia had granted Austria her independence in 1954. This meant that they had to dig up the minefields on the Austrian-Hungarian border and dismantle all the electric fences and barbed wire. All the armed patrols and stations were taken down. All that was left were the border patrols, and they had gone to Russia with the command when the revolution started. This meant that the Russian soldiers who had left often went straight over the border and into Austria. They left their posts and emigrated. The ones that managed to escape left their guns and armaments. This is how we came across a lot of our weapons, especially the tanks.

The most important thing for the revolutionaries when the uprising began was to take over the radio station and the printing works. This was where they used to print all the Russian propaganda leaflets. We needed the power of communication. This looked impossible without any heavy weaponry. The AVO and KGB officers also realised the importance of controlling the media, and they held strong defensive positions in these two buildings. The turning point was when we got the tanks. We took control of the buildings with the help of the Hungarian army. We surrounded the buildings and started firing. We never demolished the building entirely. The AVO put up a good fight, returning our fire with their machine guns, but they realised that we had superior firepower as soon as a couple of tank shells had been fired into the building. They realised that they had no chance and surrendered. We gained control of the broadcasting station and the printing works and started to do our own broadcasting. We started telling the people what was really happening.

Our prime minister had already gone, Imré Nagy. He had been replaced by Jànos Kàdar, who had been imprisoned by the AVO some time ago for trying to oppose the Hungarian communists.

Before his arrest, he was an underground leader. They had captured him as well as the Cardinal Miridzentzy. They put him in jail and tortured him so bad, that when he was released, he had hardly any finger nails or toe nails. They were forcing needles under his fingernails to try and gain information. Kadar was brought back into the government to replace Nagy, who had sought refuge in the Yugoslav embassy.

Kadar made a big mistake when he came to power by trying to tell the revolutionaries to calm down and go back to work. He assured us that the Russians were leaving and that we would have our freedom back. This was part of a big bluff as the Russians only pulled back to Romania. They were secretly assembling on the outskirts of Hungary to crush the revolution once and for all. Kadar made no attempt to defend us. Instead, we tried to ask Western countries for help with modern weapons and equipment, as we were poorly equipped to take on the Russian army. We only had leftovers from the Second World War, which just wasn't enough.

We started off using Molotov cocktails and old weapons that we had from 1945. We had rifles that had been used to train the Hungarian army. When the revolution progressed, we managed to capture some tanks. We also disarmed the dead Russian soldiers and got guns that way. The Russian equipment was more updated than our weapons, more modern. As long as the revolution lasted our weaponry became more sophisticated. We used the tanks that we had captured, and we got hold of a small amount of heavy artillery. We needed the heavy artillery if we were to capture any buildings like the radio stations. We could not take a building just by using machine guns, we could not get close enough to get inside, so we used the heavy artillery and the tanks.

When the Russians re-entered Hungary with 20 tank divisions, a lot of the soldiers were Mongolian. The Mongolian section of the Russian army was the most uneducated in the whole Russian army. My mum told me that when the Mongolians came through Tatabanya, they were spreading boot polish onto bread and eating it. They also used to boil whole chickens with the feathers still on and the insides still in them then eat them just like that. When they were crossing the river Danube in Budapest, they were asking people about the Germans. They had been told in Russia that the German army had attacked Hungary again. They were told that the Nazi's had attacked the Hungarian communists again.

The Russian Mongolians were actually looking for Germans who had left eleven years earlier when World War Two had ended. We used this lack of intelligence to trick the Mongolians. We informed them that the Germans were in a certain part of the city, and we managed to split them into two groups. We re-directed them down narrow streets where it was impossible to turn their tanks and vehicles around. These streets also had tall buildings on either side. This kind of territory was ideal for a street battle against tanks.

Because we had no modern anti-tank weapons, we had to use our wits. We let them come down the narrow streets leading into Budapest's red square. We waited until all the tanks had entered the narrow streets. They were approaching the square from two streets that were opposite each other. The young revolutionaries, little boys, and girls of different ages, then carried out the next part of our plan. What they did was to stick a Hungarian flag on the division from the East, while they left the division coming from the West alone. When the two divisions met, the first two tanks saw that one of the tanks had a Hungarian flag on it. They started to shoot each other. The revolutionaries were in and on the top of the buildings that surrounded the narrow streets. Our weaponry consisted of Molotov cocktails, which was a glass bottle filled with petrol and stuffed full of rags, which we then lit and threw. We started from the back of the tank division and worked our way to the front, throwing the bottles down onto the tanks. The streets were that narrow that the tanks could not turn round. Also, the tanks could not find the angle to shoot at us with their tanks as the streets were too narrow and the buildings too high. We were fairly safe on the top of the buildings. We knew that if we put a Hungarian flag on the tanks that they would fall for it. The Mongolians were known for being simple, and their communications were a shambles. We knew that they would struggle to keep in touch with each other. By the time they realised what was happening the damage was already done. Even if they did not fall for it we had them in the perfect place to destroy their tanks in the narrow streets.

There was a certain place that you had to aim for on the tank when you threw your Molotov cocktail. There was a two-foot plate that had inch diameter holes in it, like a grid. This was to cool down the engine. If you dropped it on this grid, the burning petrol poured into the engine and blew the tank up. We could see the turret of smoke blasting past us on its way skywards. There were not that many survivors from the tanks, as they went up that fast, the Mongolians did not have much time to get out. Those few that did escape ran towards the red square, some were on fire. We machine gunned them down from our positions on the tall buildings. They lost a lot of tanks and men in that street fight. As well as this, the street surface was quite bad. The revolutionaries had dug up the trolley bus tracks, cobblestones, and lampposts, etc. We fetched railway wagons and buses and packed them all in the street to form a barricade. This made it harder for the Russian tanks to manoeuvre.

The thing about the Russian tanks is that once they had started moving on the street, they would stop for nobody. If kids happened to cross the street, or if they were playing in the street, or if people were trying to cross the road, they wouldn't hesitate to run them over. I remember one incident when a leader took about 250 kids into a church as a safe haven as a lot of the buildings had been destroyed in the fighting. There were no windows left in a lot of the buildings in town. She took them into this big church, which was a historical monument. It was built by the Turks in the 13th century. It was made of solid stone, three foot thick, which meant it would take a bit of hammering before it would get knocked down. So she took all the kids to this church so that they would be safe. They had been living there about two or three days when the Russians started to get suspicious.

They had seen people moving in and out of the building, bringing in food and water for the kids. The Russians realised what was going on and surrounded the church with tanks. They told the leader that if they came out, they would let the kids go home to wherever they lived and that nothing would happen to them. When they finally came out, the Russians waited until all of the children were out and then they machine-gunned them down.

Later on that night, they came back with lorries and loaded all the bodies onto the lorries. They took the bodies to a cemetery in Budapest and built a mass grave using bulldozers and buried them. The mass grave was found later on by a civilian who had been to the cemetery to visit relatives. They had got suspicious when they had seen freshly turned earth and started to dig. They did the same to those children as what they did to all the political prisoners and prisoners of war in Siberia, a mass burial. Under the cover of night, they would come for the revolutionaries and civilians alike and take them away. A lot of people just disappeared in the night without explanation. They were either killed and buried in mass graves or taken to Russia or Siberia. We did not know for sure, all that we knew was that they disappeared.

Of all the leaders and figures that were well known during the revolution, I did not know a great deal about Sàndor Kopàsci or Màrk Molnàr, but I knew Pàl Maleter. He had a reputation of being a strong leader of the revolutionaries. He organised us militarily so that we knew how to fight in groups rather than individually. Also, he tried to organise the distribution of the leaflets that we were printing. He realised the importance of letting the population know the truth about the revolution on a regular basis. Before Pàl Maleter joined the revolutionaries, he was the head of a tank division in the Hungarian army. As Pal was seen as the military leader, Imrè Nagy was seen as the political leader. Imrè Nagy was the prime minister before he sought refuge at the Yugoslav embassy and replaced by Jànos Kàdar. The mistake Nagy made was to believe the Russians were really pulling out, he refused to ask Western countries for weapons and ammunition, he tried to resolve the conflict the diplomatic way. He wanted to stop the slaughter of Hungarian lives by negotiations, which never really works with the Russians. They had fooled Nagy. By the time Nagy was trying to get organised, the Russians had re-grouped on the outskirts of Hungary with another 20 tank divisions waiting to invade. As soon as they entered Hungary, the fighting started again. Eventually, they took back the radio station and started to round up the revolutionaries.

What happened when the revolution started was that all the AVO and KGB officers that had disappeared to Russia came back to Hungary dressed as civilians. They were dressed in boiler suits and general working men's clothes. The AVO offices swapped positions to remain undercover. The AVO of Budapest swapped with the AVO of Tatabànya so that no-one would recognise them in their civilian dress. They mixed with the revolutionaries and civilians. Fighting in a revolution is totally different to regular fighting. It was not like it was in the Second World War, when the enemies had distinctive uniforms, and you knew who your enemy was. In a street battle, you weren't quite sure who the enemy was, you can not pick them out in civilian dress. The most dangerous part of their plan was for the AVO and KGB officers to try and secure high positions amongst the revolutionaries. They would take charge of operations and try to lead us to fake targets. They would lead us to heavily armed Russian or AVO positions. They would lead us to the wrong part of a building or street. As soon as we got to our false targets, our fake leaders would disappear. A lot of revolutionaries got shot or killed this way.

It was hard to organise a group because you did not know who you could trust. Pàl Maleter tried to get a group together, but this was very hard because of the AVO and KGB. When the

Russians re-entered Hungary, they re-captured the print works and the radio station. Pàl Maleter and Imré Nagy sought refuge in the Yugoslav embassy, as they knew they would be safe. As soon as the Russians gained the upper hand in the revolution they tried to make a deal with Maleter and Nagy. They arranged a meeting on neutral ground to sign an agreement regarding the Russian occupation of Hungary. The deal involved giving the Hungarians their independence in a few years time. Also, to give the land back to the farmers and freedom to the population. Such was the desire for peace that Nagy and Maleter agreed to negotiate. They fell for the trick and were imprisoned and hung.

As the fighting continued, the Russians, once they came back into Hungary with greater number and force, started to gain the upper hand in the revolution. There were fewer places to hide now in Budapest, and as we were holed up in a building for the night, we didn't know, but through sheer bad luck, we were holed up opposite a house full of AVO officers. When we were coming out of the house in the morning, the AVO opened fire from the opposite side of the street. That was when I got shot. I just felt a huge bang at the back of my head, and that was the last I knew.

When I got shot, I got picked up by the Red Cross which was operated by different nationalities. There were a lot of people from Austria and a few from England in the Red Cross. When I woke up, I was outside Budapest. The Red Cross had converted an old auditorium into a specialist lung unit. The auditorium was on the top of the hills that surround Budapest. It was used mainly for people who had lung cancer. A lot of the miners were treated there who had silicone dust in their lungs and could not breathe properly. They were put in the auditorium because up there the air was cleaner. So I was in this auditorium along with a lot of other casualties from the revolution. We were in there because all the other hospitals in Budapest were also full with casualties from the revolution. The hospitals were that full that there were injured people lying in the corridors and gangways on stretchers waiting to have their wounds looked at, or to be operated on. The hospitals could not cope with the situation. Also in the cities hospitals, the Russians would come and walk up and down the corridors, and if anyone had an injury that related to the revolution, they would take them away in their lorries, and you wouldn't see them anymore. So, a lot of people were taken to this lung auditorium by the Red Cross to escape the Russians.

I had been shot in the back of my head, and I had an operation to find out the extent of the damage. I was told what the problem was, but they said that they didn't have the time to take the shrapnel out. It is still there to this day. They told me that as soon as I got back to Tatabanya that I was to go to the hospital and have the shrapnel taken out. They could not treat me there, as there were people in a far worse state than me. We had heard what the Russians were doing to the other hospitals in Budapest so all of us who were in a fit enough state to travel and were connected to the revolution left before the Russians could come for us. Before I left for Tatabanya, I was given a document by the Red Cross. This document said that I had been in the auditorium having my lungs filled with oxygen, and I had been convalescing from this treatment. This was because it was very difficult to move around in the streets without ID. The Russians checked on everybody, and you had to have a good reason to be on the street. It took me around two or three days of walking in the streets before I could get to the train station. The streets were almost un-walkable, never mind attempting to drive a car down them. I think the streets were worse than in 1945 when the Second World War had finished.

I had great difficulty getting home after I had left the hospital. There were no trains running, no engines, no wagons, or railway. When I was at the train station I had to hang around and wait for any vehicle that was available, that was going to Tatabànya on the roads that were not demolished. This was hard as un-demolished roads were few and far between. Anyway, I finally managed to get a lift. There was a small lorry that was taking some supplies to the hospital in Tatabànya, and I got a lift with him. It was a worrying time waiting in the train station. I was there for eight hours and throughout that time the Russian soldiers were coming in and searching the station every hour or so. They were sometimes in pairs or sometimes there was half a dozen of them, but they never left empty handed. They always left with people who they had taken from the platform who were trying to leave Budapest.

When I got home, I went straight to the hospital and told them about my injury. I told them what the doctors had said in Budapest and that the shrapnel had to be removed. So they sent me upstairs, and I went to see a surgeon. He felt the wound, X-rayed it and then froze it. He sent me to the waiting room and asked me to return when I was called. The surgeon said that it was not a long operation. He just had to cut the flesh and extract the shrapnel with a magnet. So I went upstairs to the waiting room. While I was waiting, I just happened to look out of the window which overlooked the hospital gardens around the back of the building. I saw six Russian tanks pull up plus a lot of soldiers. They started to make their way to the hospital entrance. About five minutes later, they came out of the hospital carrying stretchers with people on them. They just put the stretcher on the floor beside the tank, got hold of the injured person and chucked them onto the body of the tank and drove off. When I saw what

was happening, I never said anything to anyone,
I just got up and left and went home. When I
was walking down our street, I met my next door
neighbour. He was a pensioner, an old timer who
was against communism from start to finish. He
told me that the man who lived over the road
from us told him that as soon as the revolution
had quietened down, I would be the first person
to be shot. The bloke over the road was a big
communist who was the Managing Director of the
Tatabanyan aluminium industry. This news was
enough for me. When I got into the house, I told
my dad that I had decided to leave Hungary.

## My Escape to Austria

*"I remember one day when we were walking near the border, we saw an entire family get gunned down. The husband, wife and little boy, who was about 5 years old."*

## Chapter Five - *My Escape to Austria*

The same night that I decided to leave Hungary, I went down to see two of my friends who I used to work with, and I persuaded them to leave as well. So the following morning at about 6am, we set off. When I first told my mum and dad that I had decided to leave, my dad stayed neutral. He did not tell me to stay or go. If he told me to go and I got caught, he would blame himself for telling me to go. If I got caught, I would have been killed or sent to Siberia. He did not tell me to stay either, because if my friends had escaped, then he thought I would blame him for persuading me to stay. So my mum packed me up some food to last a couple of days.

We left that morning, and we walked down to the railway station and waited for a train. In the waiting room, there were a lot of people waiting for the same train, which was going towards Hegyeshalom. This was the border town between

Hungary and Austria. Meanwhile, as we were waiting for the train, the Russian soldiers were patrolling. They kept coming into the station, have a look round, then they would take some people away. Then they would come back and do the same thing again. We were very anxious for the train to arrive so we could get away. When the train eventually arrived, it was packed. It was a steam train pulling around 25 carriages. By the time we got on, we could hardly move for all the people. Everybody was going to Hegyeshalom, the border town. It seemed that all of a sudden, everyone had a relative in Hegyeshalom. The real reason was that everyone on the train was trying to escape. The Russians knew it, but they did not do anything about it there and then. Their plan was to wait until we got to Hegyeshalom. The border town was already surrounded by two tank divisions. Anyone who got off in Hegyeshalom train station was detained, and they would have their passports taken off of them, then let go.

When the Russians had the passports, no-one could get out of the country, plus they had the names and addresses of everyone who was trying to flee. Having obtained the names, the Russians could wait until the heat of the revolution had died down, then they could come and collect them. We stopped at another two or three stations and picked up even more passengers. It was that packed that there were people lying in the luggage racks above the seats. You could barely get a matchstick between the people there were that many on the train.

About 20 miles from Hegyeshalom the train was stopped. By this time, it was dark outside, it was around 5.30 - 6.00pm. It was 11th November when I left, so it was well into Winter already. In some places, there was already snow on the ground. We did not know why the train had been stopped, but we saw the driver making his way through the crowds. He came down the carriages, and when he got to us, we realised what he was doing. He and his mate who stoked the fire were carrying a big sack. They were collecting all the money from the passengers. They told us that if we were lucky enough to escape, we would not need our Hungarian money. They also told us that if we were caught we also wouldn't need our money as we would be shot or imprisoned. We gave them all our money and he told us that he had his train set up. The carriages behind the engine that carried the coal, fuel and water, had a secret compartment made out of wood in the middle of all the coal. He said that he was going to put his family in the compartment and cross the border with his family and his train. So, we all got off the train. He showed us two red lights, which was the radio station in Hegyeshalom. These were the pilot lights on top of the building, as it was about 200 feet high. He told us that he had been fetching thousands each day, and he had good connections with people who would take us over the border. He told us to make sure that we were between the two pilot lights. The Russians had dug in either side of the two lights. The Russian border patrol was mainly reinforcements, because when the revolution started all the border patrols had either escaped into Austria or left their posts. But by now they had reinforced the border patrols as they knew that a lot of Hungarians would try to escape.

We followed the driver's instructions and started walking. There were hundreds of us if not thousands. There were quite a few families amongst us who had kids, so they had a lot of luggage. But my two friends and I had nothing but a bit of food, we did not bring any suitcases. So we were helping the people who were struggling with luggage or with their kids. We managed to get through the forests while keeping our eyes on the two pilot lights. We got to a village where we were met by some men. They told us not to go any further now. The scouts who were going to take us across the border were already taking a big group across the border. The half a dozen men had taken around 5,000 to the border, and they would not be back until the morning. They could not take us during the day as it was too dangerous. The Russians shoot on sight during the day. But at night time the scouts told us that there wouldn't be any problems unless we virtually bumped into them. They would not come out and patrol at night. So we had to try and cross into Austria at night.

We waited in the village all day, they put us up in big barns, where they used to keep all the livestock. We could not go out on the streets, in case the Russian patrols saw us. They gave us food and drink and told us not to go out into the streets to look around as the Russians knew how many people lived in that village and if they saw any obvious extra numbers, they would realise what was happening. They were frightened that they would get shot as well if they found out that they were taking us across the border. So we waited until night time until the scouts came back. They divided us up into the groups, and we started off for the border. It was pitch black, and we had to travel through a forest.

We had to keep as quiet as possible in case the Russians were patrolling the woods at night. There wasn't much chance of this as the Russian soldiers were scared to come out at night. We were travelling for about four to five hours when we came to a point where the Russians were dug in. There were rolls of barbed wire and trenches. Beyond this there was a strip of land about 20 yards wide, it was nicely raked. It was a very fine soil and beyond that there were little holes. We knew that this was the border because in 1954 when the Russians left Austria, they had to take up all the barbed wire and dig up the mine field.

The Austrian farmers were complaining that they were losing cattle and men because of the disused mine field. We knew that we were in Austria because the farmers fields were cut into strips, not like in Hungary. The fields were in two or three-acre strips and between the fields there was flat stone so that the farmers could tell their own land and not get it mixed up with their neighbour's land.

When we got through the farmers field, we hit upon a cobblestone road. Along the roadside there were trees that had some bark removed and the Austrian flag had been painted on it. Also, we saw that they had flagstone markers that showed the distance between towns. We never had these in Hungary. Out of nowhere, we saw flashing blue lights appear on the roadside. We saw that they were police lorries. Everyone ran for cover into the ditches that were by the roadside. I knew as soon as I saw the blue lights that they didn't belong to any communist vehicles. The AVO vehicles had red lights, and the border patrol had green lights. Hungary had no border vehicles that had blue lights. We then heard a voice shouting out 'God Muggen Austria,' which meant 'Good

Morning Austria.' We knew then that we were in Austria.

They put us in lorries that were waiting for us and they took us to the Red Cross where we got hot coffee, tea, and sandwiches. In that town most of the properties had barns. The churches, schools, and farms, etc. all had barns that had been cleaned out and the floor had been covered in straw. There were a lot of blankets that had been supplied by the Red Cross, courtesy of other countries. We stayed in this town for about two or three days. I cannot really describe how I was feeling, other than I was unbelievably happy. It was like somebody who had been jailed for life was suddenly told that they were free to go. I really liked Austria. Because it was part of the Austro-Hungarian Empire before the First World War, most Austrians could speak Hungarian. We were taken out every morning and evening to different people's houses for a meal. The Austrian people would also take us out for meals and to play football and things like that. They also took us to the cinema to see films. This was a first for me as all I ever saw at the cinema in Hungary was films and documentaries about propaganda. Stuff about how one farm or pit was outperforming another. We had never seen any Western cinema, so it was good to watch cowboy films, which I really liked. You never got this in Hungary. Being in Austria was a very nice experience, a very happy one.

We all heard the following day that the train driver had made it through. He had got the steam engine up to full speed, which was about 60 – 70 miles per hour and headed towards the border. On the border, there were two Russian tanks across the railway track plus a barricade. This was where the train was supposed to stop, and the Russian soldiers were to come aboard and check all the passports. If you didn't have a passport or a good reason to go to Austria, they would not let you go. The train driver first brought his last load of passengers to the same place where he had dropped us off, about 20 miles from the border. He then got the train up to full speed. There were only him and his mate in the engine, his family was in the specially prepared carriage behind the engine. He got the train up to full speed and smashed through the tanks and barricades.

We saw a picture in the newspaper in the town that we were staying in. The two tanks were overturned. When he smashed through, the tanks had started shooting. They did not get the engine as that had already passed through, but all the empty carriages, there was nothing left. We found out that the following day, the Austrian government had handed the train back to the Hungarian border patrol. There was a news article about it in the Austrian papers. We were there for about a week, and we used to go for a walk around the town. We would see people trying to escape during the daytime across the forest. We would watch them trying to make a dash for it, one or two at a time, but as soon as they got into the clearing where the minefield used to be, they just got shot.

They used to rake the disused minefield every day so they would know if anyone had tried to cross it because of the fresh footprints. I remember one day when we were walking near the border, we saw an entire family get gunned down. The husband, wife, and little boy, who was about five years old. Every day dozens got shot. They tried to come across unorganised. They could not be bothered to wait until it was night or for the scouts to guide them across. They were too impatient.

After about a week, they took us from Rohonc to Graz, which was a big town. I think there used to be a concentration camp there during the war. We stayed at Graz for another week when we were visited by an official from the NCB. He had an interpreter and got us all together and told us that the National Coal Board wanted around 20,000 Hungarians to go to England to work in the mining industry. The official was asking for proof from the people who claimed to be miners. I still had my papers and qualifications that I gained from the mining college. I gave them my papers and my passport and that was the last I saw of them. They said that we would hear from them in a couple of days. We had to move out of Graz because there were that many refugees coming in that there was not enough room. They were desperate to ship us anywhere in the world that could use our skills. About three days later the official told me to get my belongings together. A convoy of lorries and buses came and drove us to Linz. This city had an airport. There were private planes waiting for us. These were piloted by voluntary American and English pilots. I was on my way to England.

# My New Life in England

*"The people accepted us in Mexborough, but there was a bit of controversy about us working down the mines. I could understand how they felt because we could not speak much English."*

## Chapter Six - *My New Life in England*

We landed in Nettlestone on the 8th of December 1956. We landed at night time and from the airport, we were taken to a big army camp on buses that were provided.

The British Army at this time were involved in the Suez crisis, so the only Army personnel that were left were the cooks and the cleaners. There were around 50 of them. We arrived at this camp which was a massive place. The room that I stayed in had around 22 refugees in it. There were beds either side and in the middle of the room there was a great big fireplace with wooden chairs and tables all around it. One of the Army lads used to come every morning and clean it out. He would then build up the fire with about five or six bucket fulls of coal. It was a massive fire. They had a big canteen there, and the food was fantastic. We could have as much as we wanted. For breakfast we could have eggs, fried, boiled, or scrambled, fried potatoes, bacon, sausage, tomatoes, and beans. You could have cereal as well, and there was always toast and marmalade on the table if you wanted it. We had three meals a day. Breakfast, lunch, and supper, which was around 7pm.

There was a big washroom with lots of showers. We could shower every day, which was a luxury after all the travelling. The Army lads would cut our hair whenever we wanted it. There was a great big recreation room where we could play snooker or watch television. It was the first time that I had seen a television. I also used to listen to the radio for a special reason. When I left Hungary, I told my mum that I could not write home. This was because my letters would be intercepted by the secret police and that meant that my mum and dad would be imprisoned. So before I left the Red Cross said that they were setting up a secret code system. This was so all the people fleeing Hungary could contact their relatives by using the code they knew that their relation had made it out safely. I told my mum and dad that my code was 'The Eagle.' The reason I chose 'The Eagle' was because of a local legend in my hometown of Tatabanya.

In Tatabanya there is a massive monument of an eagle perched on top of a huge limestone rock. The eagle is carved out of about fifty tonnes of solid bronze. It was made in the 13th century by the Turks when they were occupying Hungary. Underneath the statue, there is a cave. During the Turkish occupation, the Hungarians used to use the cave to hide in. If anyone happened to die in the cave, they would be chucked out of the cave. Every time this happened, an eagle would swoop down and feed on the remains. The Turks kept noticing the eagles swooping down to feed on the bodies and they soon realised where the Hungarians were hiding. The Turks set the cave on fire, and everybody was burnt alive. For the memory of the legend, they erected the statue of the eagle. So a lot of us were going into the rec room every day to listen to the Red Cross broadcasts. I had been going there for about five or six days when I heard my secret code. This made me very happy as I knew that if my mum and dad were listening, they would know that I was alive and made it.

As I recall, I think Nettlestone was a seaside resort because we would walk for about two miles before coming to a resort. We would walk down the promenade, and we would see hotels and bed and breakfasts. We would meet up with the local boys and girls from this resort, and we would play football and hang around together. They would take us into the arcades and cinemas at night. They also used to take us to their homes for a meal. They would buy us stuff like fruit and chocolates. We did not have much fruit or chocolates in Hungary. We would be given ten shillings pocket money a week each, which was a lot of money for us. The shopkeepers were understanding whenever we went to buy anything. They would take the right money out of our hands and give us the correct change. I used to go to the cinema most nights.

We all had a good time in Nettlestone. We picked up the English language as we went along. The kids taught us English, and we taught them Hungarian just by asking questions. We used a lot of sign language to start off with, but as time went on we started to understand each other. We knew that we didn't have to learn English to get a job because we came to England to be miners. We already had jobs to go to. Nettlestone was just a temporary place where we stayed until we got moved to the towns where we were supposed to go. We were at Nettlestone for a fortnight, then we went to Tidworth, which was another Army camp. We were at Tidworth for about a fortnight. The English people were the same in Tidworth as they were in Nettlestone. They were very friendly, giving us food and inviting us to their homes for meals and things like that.

My friend and I got invited to a house for Christmas dinner. The parents had two sons and one daughter, and they were all at college. They showed us a lot of books and dictionaries. My friend and I used to sit for hours trying to find the words that we wanted to use. It was the first time in my life that I had seen a dinner table set like that. They had a china dinner service and silverware, they must have been well off. I think they were in the hotel business. We would meet up with the local teenagers like we did in Nettlestone and they would take us out. They would take us to the cinemas, arcades, and fairs. They would pay for us on all the rides. As far as I could see, they had a lot of money.

From Tidworth, we went by boat to London, then by train to Victoria. The NCB paid for us to stay in different hotels. There were thousands of us. We stayed in the hotels overnight and had a good meal and a good night's sleep. In the morning we went by bus to the train station and headed to Doncaster. When we got to Doncaster, we got a bus to Mexborough. At Mexborough, there was a hostel especially set up for the miners. It was not first class accommodation, but it was warm with central heating, and the furniture was good. It did not look very good from the outside, but inside it was very comfortable.

The people accepted us in Mexborough, but there was a bit of controversy about us working down the mines. I could understand how they felt because we could not speak much English. Before we could go down the mine, we had to have training. But you could not have the training if you could not speak English. All the instructions down the mines were in English, so it was very dangerous for anyone who couldn't speak English to be down the mines. The NCB sent us to school for five days a week to learn to speak English. What they did as well was to give us seven pounds and ten shillings a week wages.

Which was a lot. But because speaking English was so important they would take a day's wages off you if you missed a day at school. It was like if you missed a shift at work, you would get docked that day's pay.

We got put onto groups, twelve pupils to one teacher. The NCB brought the teachers in from all over England. Our teacher was a woman named Ms. Jeeves, she was from London. She could speak four different languages. English, French, German and Italian. Our school was a Sunday school building in the church grounds. We used to go there five days a week to learn English. But it was impossible to learn English in school as we were all Hungarian except for the teacher. The only way to learn was to mix with the English people and to break away from the Hungarians altogether. When we went to school we had a good laugh and got on well with the teacher but after four weeks the teacher was speaking Hungarian nearly as well as us, and we were speaking hardly any English. It was hard to learn because when we got back from school we were all together in the hostel, so we only ever spoke Hungarian.

When we got back to school the next day, we had forgotten all the new words that we had learned as we weren't practising them in the hostel. After about four months I knew the coal board wouldn't accept any of us as miners as we couldn't speak English. I could have been in the hostel for about ten or twenty years and still not got a job. There were just too many of us to put down the mines at that point as well. So I made a decision to find a different job with the help of an interpreter. He gave me the address of the International Harvesters in Doncaster. They made tractors, combined harvesters, and farm machinery. The interpreter wrote down the directions on how to get to Doncaster and the Harvesters and gave me the bus fare. So I went to International Harvesters and luckily I got the job.

I went back to the hostel and told the interpreter and the next day he said he would come back to Doncaster and help me to find a place to lodge. I moved in with a Ukrainian couple, so I had broken away from all the Hungarians in Mexborough. The Ukrainian couple had been here since 1945 and could only speak about as much English as I could, so I only stopped there a couple of months.

At work I was in the press shop, working on a 350-ton press. My foreman liked me because I was a good worker and regular timekeeper. I was only there a month when I was entrusted to do my own setting on my machine. I was working from office blueprints and setting up all sorts of different jobs. At dinner times and at tea breaks I used to sit down and listen to the other workers. By asking for tools and equipment plus the general conversation that goes on during the working day, all helped me with my English.

From living with the Ukrainian couple, I

moved in with a Hungarian couple in Childers Street. I only stayed there for a fortnight as I did not like it. They were constantly speaking Hungarian, and I wanted to speak English. I wanted to try and pick up the English language as quickly as possible because I knew that I had a better chance of getting a job. I knew I had to learn the language in order make a new life for myself in England. So from there I went to Morley Road in Wheatley, Doncaster. I bought myself a motorbike, a 600 Matchless. I used to go to work on my motorbike. At the weekend my friends and I used to go to different places on our bikes. We went to places like York and the seaside. I was working regular nights for three years at the Harvesters as I preferred nights. As well as getting more money for working nights it worked out better for me as during the day I liked looking around the town as it was all new to me. I liked to discover new things.

I had been in England two years when I wrote

home for the first time. I was waiting for my friends to write home first and when I knew that they had got a reply from their relatives, I knew it was alright to write to my parents. This was because they usually punished the relatives of any Hungarian that had escaped. It was 1958 when I first wrote home, this made my parents very happy because they never got my secret code. The Russians had set up a system that muffled any Western broadcast to Hungary. So my parent's radio was suffering from interference, and they could not hear my secret code word. My mum and dad were overjoyed that I was alright, but my sister had mixed feelings, as when I left Tatabanya I did not say goodbye to her. This was because of the simple reason that if I woke her to say goodbye, she would want to come with me. It would have been a hard decision to make. To take your sister with you when you were not sure what would happen to yourself. It was not like visiting friends or going on holiday, it was a life or death decision.

While I was working at the Harvesters, a lot of the Hungarians started to get unruly. They would go out at night and pick fights with the English lads. There were a lot of stabbings and a lot of trouble caused by a minority of the Hungarians. That is one of the reasons why I never mixed with them. I just stayed at home, or if I did go out at night, I would keep away from them. After two or three years in Doncaster dozens of them had been jailed because of their violent nature. I did not like this so I never bothered with them.

Out of the two friends that I escaped with, I lost one of them as soon as I got off the train. There were that many people and it was very dark. But I have found out since that he went to America. As far as I know, he has got his own building business, as he was a bricklayer. The last time I heard from him, he told me that he had broken his ankle while surfing in America. My other friend came to England with me, but when we got to Nettlestone we got put in different groups, and I lost him. I have had no contact with him since, but I know that he is in England.

When I was at Morley Road, I met my wife. She used to live near me, and I can remember looking out of my window and watching her ride her bike around the block carrying her little sister on the handlebars. I met her in October 1958, and I was invited to her house for Christmas dinner. A little while later I was lodging there. I bought my own furniture, and they gave me a room. I was sleeping in the same room as my wife's brother. I was there for a couple of years, so my English really picked up. I got engaged, and two years later I was married in 1962.

My new life had started in England, but my old life in Hungary could never be forgotten.